A GARDEN FROM

A HUNDRED PACKETS

OF SEED

A GARDEN FROM
A HUNDRED PACKETS
OF SEED

JAMES FENTON

FARRAR, STRAUS AND GIROUX

NEW YORK

Farrar, Straus and Giroux
19 Union Square West, New York 10003

This book is based on a series of articles that first appeared in *The Guardian*. The author thanks Annalena McAfee and Alice Munsey.

Grateful acknowledgment is made for permission to reprint excerpts from "Bavarian Gentians," from *The Complete Poems of D. H. Lawrence*, edited by V. De Sola Pinto & F. W. Roberts, copyright © 1964, 1971 by Angela Ravagli and C. M. Weekly, Executors of the Estate of Frieda Lawrence Ravagli. Used by permission of Viking Penguin, a division of Penguin Putnam Inc.

Library of Congress Cataloging-in-Publication Data
Fenton, James, 1949–
    A Garden from a hundred packets of seed / James
Fenton.— 1st American ed.
        p.   cm.
    ISBN 0-374-16029-5 (hardcover : alk. paper)
    1. Gardening. I. Title.

SB455 .F46 2002
635'.9—dc21

                                            2001054452

Designed by Jonathan D. Lippincott

www.fsgbooks.com

1   3   5   7   9   10   8   6   4   2

To Michael Collins

without whom there would be no garden

CONTENTS

Introduction   3

1. Flowers and Their Colors   13
2. Flowers for Their Size   23
3. Flowers That Hop Around   31
4. Flowers for Cutting   39
5. The Perennial Prejudice   47
6. Useful and Decorative Herbs   55
7. The Micro-Meadow   63
8. The Poppy Festival   75
9. Climbers on Impulse   83
10. For the Tropical Look   91
11. As an Afterthought   99
12. The Rest of the Kit   107
    When Raising Plants from Seed   113
    The Seed List   117

A GARDEN FROM

A HUNDRED PACKETS

OF SEED

INTRODUCTION

 OF COURSE, you may say it is only a game, and indeed it *is* a game: a game of lists. What plants would you choose to grow, given a blank slate of a garden, and given the stipulation that everything you grow in this garden must be raised by you from seed? It is a game of choice, but it could be more than a game. At the very least, it could be a way of thinking afresh about how to put a garden together, and with what purpose in mind.

For years now the gardening press (newspaper columns, magazines, and glossy books) has been, consciously and unconsciously, campaigning for a common approach. One starts with a design, the "bones" of the garden, the "structure." Next one shades in plausible areas and shapes, indicating trees, shrubs, and perennials. Finally, one is supposed to go out and buy the plants penciled in in those plausible shapes. The rest is mostly maintenance.

This approach to gardening would never have become plausible or popular if it did not reflect a certain wisdom. But may I respectfully suggest that it is not the only way to garden? It may be one wise way to operate, but it is not the only wisdom available to humankind. To take the simplest counterexample: in Britain every town has several communal gardens in which one can rent assigned plots known as allotments; these are used mainly for growing vegetables and fruit; an allotment gardener does not have to start with a design. The important question is: What do I want to grow?

The design of an allotment is hardly an issue. Content is everything. So the allotment gardener in January may be happily and appropriately engaged in the simple act of compiling lists: this is what I want to eat this year, or this is what I want to grow for the challenge, or this is what has piqued my curiosity.

Why should the flower gardener not feel the same? Why should he or she not ask: What do I feel like growing this year? What delights me? What bores me? What is ravishing? What is revolting? Flower fanatic and vegetable fiend, we are seated at the same kitchen table, leafing through many of the same catalogues. The same gales are howling around the rooftops. The same frosts are glazing the water butts. Why should I not feel, this January, the same freedom as my pea epicurean, my marrow-maniacal friend?

The first answer that springs to mind is that a flower garden is of its nature a permanent thing, whereas an allotment, to all intents and purposes, closes down for the winter. But this objection need not necessarily hold. After all, I have not yet defined the sort of flower garden I am thinking of. Indeed, I do not want to define it at all too nicely, because I am ambitious to hold the attention of more than one kind of reader (including, of course, the allotment gardener).

So my definition—my nondefinition—of a garden must include a spectacular one that I saw last summer in Manhattan, which consisted of nothing but morning glories grown on a fire escape, high up above the street. Mustard and cress sown on a washcloth, Virginia stock in an old crab shell, or a row of hyacinths in glasses—

all these count as gardens, in my understanding of the word, along with Great Dixter, Powis Castle, and Versailles.

For those who have landed on some property of which they can say, "This is where I hope to live for the next so-many years," I have some advice, which may prove welcome, since it may well prove cheap. It is *not* the case that your permanent plantings, your graph-paper layout of shrubs and perennials (supposing this to be your ultimate goal), should be put in place as soon as possible. If you are renovating an old garden, or starting one from scratch, it may well be good practice to plant experimentally for a couple of seasons, relying mainly on annuals, until the soil has been well conditioned and the perennial weeds have been largely defeated.

The larger the garden, the more welcome this practice will be. Your shrubs and your perennials may take time to bulk up, whereas your annuals are by definition going to perform in one season. But that is not the end of the story. Many annuals will make a permanent contribution to the garden by seeding themselves around. The smaller ones may find their way into nooks and crannies where it would have been hard to plant them in the first place. The larger ones may, if given a chance, make impressive colonies, in the way that opium poppies do. So they will come back in profusion year after year.

But of course not every would-be gardener has the prospect of owning or occupying the same plot of ground for a large number of years. One moves on. One moves up in the world. One moves *down* in the world. One comes home and finds the locks changed and one's luggage on the street. Not everyone wants to lavish the same expenditure on a small garden as on a small kitchen (although it is amazing how often the designers of small gardens will work on this assumption, allowing a budget of £12,000 to put in that "bone structure").

This list is not only about annuals. It looks at any sort of plant that can be appropriately grown from seed. I do not propose that you start your roses in this way: that would be, as Peter Pan says of death, an awfully *big* adventure. But I aim to devise a diverse and interesting starter kit for a garden, balancing the obvious (but irresistible) with the more recherché.

As for the design of this flower garden, I insist on keeping it vague. A hundred varieties of flower might look cramped on a balcony, spectacular in a situation only one size up from there. For it is amazing what can be crammed into a small space. Conversely, it is amazing the number of plants that could, in theory, be raised from so large a number as a hundred packets of seed.

I think that the proposed garden should, on the whole, be fairly sunny; and perhaps it should have some soil. But if the soil is an utter write-off, there is time to think of railway ties and raised beds. In my previous garden, I struggled with clay and builders' rubble. One day a friend, an expert gardener, came to see my efforts. They were pitiable. My friend told me to buy railway ties, put weed killer on what I had so far, and build raised beds, importing the soil for them and making no attempt to reform the soil I had.

I listened to what he was telling me in some dismay, and I ignored his advice. But I remembered it all the second time around, when I moved to a derelict farm and proceeded to lay out a garden on all kinds of not entirely promising terrain. I no longer believed that subsoil would, in the course of a few seasons, magically transform itself into topsoil. Where soil was needed, we imported it, along with manure, grit, sand, and compost from mushroom farms (a useful source of bulky organic material): piles and piles of the stuff have been required over the years, but that is because we have been working on an ambitious scale.

But even with an average town garden, if

you have to import soil, buy it in bulk, rather than by the bag. It is depressing how many bags you would need to fill a modest raised bed, and it is astonishing how much can be spent during a quick, impatient trip to a garden center. Conversely, it is gratifying to see how costs can be reduced by sensible bulk buying.

But this is not a book about huge projects. It is about thinking your way towards an essential flower garden, by the most traditional of routes: planting some seeds and seeing how they grow. The seeds I have chosen are generally speaking ones which have, over several years, given me pleasure in my garden. This is my personal anthology.

ONE

FLOWERS
AND THEIR COLORS

FIRST AND FOREMOST, flowers attract us by their colors. But of course it is not us they are trying so hard to attract: it is the birds, the butterflies, the insects, and those legendary night-pollinating moths. If a flower garden gives me the impression that it is flowering there for my pleasure and benefit, it is engaged in a deception. And if I fall for that deception, I am like someone who, entering a crowded room, believes that all eyes are upon him, when in fact all eyes are upon the swarm of bees visible just over his shoulder.

"How beautiful are the retired flowers!" wrote Keats in a famous passage; "how they would lose their beauty were they to throng into the highway crying out, 'admire me I am a violet! dote upon me I am a primrose!' " In fact that is exactly what the flowers, even the retired flowers, are saying to their pollinators. Or, if not that, then they are saying something coarser.

And their colors, which provoke in us such a profound and complex response, were once their exclusive property. No one saw such colors, unless it was in a flower, or a gemstone, or some extraordinary artifice such as purple-dyed cloth. Some flowers may have disturbed or repelled by their mysterious or obscene shapes, but none, surely, were thought ugly for their colors. Sad, perhaps. But never ugly.

Today some makers of gardens are so brow-beaten by color snobbery that they settle for a garden in which all flowers are excluded, or they take nervous care to check which flowers, which colors, are okay. Gardening writers, in the hope of giving the weight of science to their reflections, talk about combinations of complementary colors, and sometimes even refer to the color wheel. But this is uncandid taste masquerading as high theory.

There is no point in asking, in the abstract, whether burnt orange will look good alongside vermilion. A garden is not a canvas, and even with a canvas the question has no answer. How large a patch of burnt orange, in relation to how large a patch of vermilion—and what else is going on within the proposed color field? Is the gardener who thinks of placing a burnt-orange flower beside a vermilion one taking into account the color and relative importance of the leaves? Or is it assumed that all greens are some-how factored out by the retina?

Gardening is quite unlike painting, but there are things one can learn from the painter never-theless. John Gage, the great historian of color theory, tells a story of Turner and Constable ex-hibiting their paintings side by side in 1832 in the crowded conditions of Somerset House. Painters in these exhibitions (and Turner in particular) specialized in last-minute tricks to ensure that their works looked well.

On this occasion Constable found "the red robes of the dignitaries in his picture of the *Opening of Waterloo Bridge* (London, National Gallery) cast into obscurity by the wafer of red sealing-wax which Turner applied to the water of his cool green sea-piece next to it, *Helvoet-sluys*, and later painted into the form of a buoy. 'He has been here,' said Constable when he saw it, 'and fired a gun.' "

Some small flowers possess this ability to "fire a gun." #1, Pheasant's Eye, the hardy annual *Adonis aestivalis*, is a flower with the force of a concentrated blood-red anemone—a small ranunculus, in other words. The kind of flower you would expect to find in a Mughal miniature, or in the border of a Book of Hours. You give it a place to grow. It comes back year after year, an unerring shot.

And in such company who could object to the classic Cornflower, *Centaurea cyanus*, #2, a flower more often seen in the shops these days than ever before. The gardener should not be too proud to learn from the florist, or to plant what is so obviously beautiful people forget to recommend it—in this case, the flower which defined a certain range of blue.

I intend soon (taking a tip from the florist's bucket) to try out #3, the Safflower, *Carthamus tinctorius*, whose other name, the Saffron Thistle, reminds us what it is—that orange thistle which sometimes, on reaching London, seems to have had too crushing a ride.

It is the full orange I want, no lame excuse for a hue. People are sometimes under the illusion that the flowers they find ugly, or overassertive, are the ones that have been genetically modified. In point of fact, the flowers they find ugly are very often orange, like the incomparable #4, California Poppy, *Eschscholzia californica*. When I first invited visitors to my garden, they turned the corner and very loudly and flatly declared, "I don't like *that*." Perhaps I had let it seed itself too promiscuously, but I have charted its favor in the last decade. Today I think people would say, more tactfully, "Orange can sometimes be so difficult to *place*."

It means the same thing. It means, I don't like orange: it "fires a gun." But I remember one summer, in the august Venetian courtyard of the Isabella Stewart Gardner Museum in Boston, all the window boxes had been filled with trailing #5, Nasturtiums, *Tropaeolum majus*, the seed we are given to plant as children because it is large enough to handle individually: it is childproof. Presented so assertively and in such numbers, the nasturtiums dismissed any doubts about their worthiness.

For this list I choose the admirable "Alaska" with its variegated leaves, and no two leaves ever the same; each one a masterpiece. In my garden we try to accommodate any variety of nasturtium we can find. Some we grow from seed, some from tubers. Nor do I like a year to pass without the orange lollipop flowers of the tall #6, Mexican Sunflower, *Tithonia rotundifolia.* "The Torch" is the full-size variety. I first became aware of it on a visit to Monet's garden at Giverny, but I have no idea whether Monet would actually have grown it. The striking thing about Monet's garden—the part of it which fronts the house, not the water garden—is its brightness, its obviousness.

And you see how obvious my taste is. I like a flower the color of blue poster paint, #7, *Phacelia campanularia*, the California Bluebell; of the purest lemon yellow like #8, *Oenothera biennis*, the Evening Primrose. I like the plants of childhood, like #9, Love-in-a-Mist, *Nigella damascena*, and #10, Forget-Me-Not, *Myosotis sylvatica*. This leaves us so far notably short on reds and pinks, but not chronically short with ninety more to go.

TWO

FLOWERS
FOR THEIR SIZE

"I LOVE FLOWERS," says a friend, "but I don't like *plants*." I can easily understand the distinction. Plants involve mess and responsibility and edaphic ("of or pertaining to the soil") requirements. They perhaps expect a commitment of us that we are not, at this stage in our lives, prepared to give. Flowers can seem to come out of nowhere. Bought, arranged, admired, chucked out—they are given no chance to reproach us. Arum lilies are like this: spotless, exotic, unreal. One can tell from his photographs that Robert Mapplethorpe loved flowers. One hardly expects him to have liked plants.

Among the plants for people who don't really like plants is the recently popular category called "architectural." What is an architectural plant? It is something big, and possibly expensive, and of a bold shape—above all something that promises to make an immediate and permanent impact on the space we are filling—but its resemblance to actual architecture may be minimal. A stand of bamboo does not remind me of any architecture I know, even though I have lived in countries where much of the architecture uses bamboo. And what building looks like a phormium?

If I gaze up at a giant hogweed (*Heracleum mantegazzianum*, a plant which we may not grow—an irresponsible plant), I may indeed be reminded of Gothic fan vaulting. But a giant hogweed is not an architectural plant in the popular sense, because by the end of the year it is going to let us down: this beautiful structure will die back. I might add that if the giant hogweed looks architectural in its structure, then so do many umbellifers of different scale: cow parsley, dill, and (a crop failure for us last year) *Ammi majus,* which is referred to in one of my books as false bishop's weed. (False bishops! When have you ever met a bishop who wasn't false?)

Still, if we are to be thwarted in our ambitions to have the giant hogweed romping around the periphery, the angelicas are there as our reward, the grand old sentinels of vegetable gardens. I would choose #11, the Oriental *Angelica gigas*, purple-stemmed and purple-flowered, although we have found it to be monocarpic (that is, it dies after flowering).

In general, experimenting with various angelicas, we have found them easiest to keep going by shaking the seeds out of the ripe seed heads and allowing them to grow where they fall (they do not remain viable long). A plant, then, which may take a couple of years to reach full size. There follows one summer of glory, before it goes over. Such a habit cannot easily be accommodated in the kind of garden in which every scrap of space is supposed to be maximally active, year in, year out.

All those umbels, all those umbellules . . . My garden is the subject of crazes, but with an underlying tendency towards the encyclopedic. So the umbellifer craze makes an investment of time and space in #12, the Giant Fennel, *Ferula communis*, obligatory, given the prospect of an eventual (they say) five-meter flower spike (only likely under Mediterranean conditions). I am warned that it may be advisable to remove this spike before large amounts of seed are set, to keep the plant perennial. But what we want from such plants is the spectacle they offer as they go, so we must pay for this.

With anything that grows really, really fast

and large in a temperate climate, there is likely to be a price to pay. A ceanothus will romp up a wall, but its wood and its roots will be vulnerable to wind. The wonderfully obliging #13, *Abutilon vitifolium*, which is a ten-foot-tall woody mallow, coming with white or lavender flowers, similarly produces a wood which needs the protection of a wall. After a few years, although the stem is thick at the base, the whole becomes overdeveloped and ungainly. If something puts on six foot of growth in a year, one cannot expect that growth to be of the quality of, say, teak. The abutilon makes a bargain with us: it grows fast, and can easily be replaced from its own seed. But it does need replacing—it is not "architectural."

When I look at #14, the Shoo-Fly Plant, *Nicandra physalodes*, growing self-sown in the surface of my drive, with its feet in ballast over concrete rubble over clay, I think to myself:

Somewhere in the world this thing must be an utter menace. Peru is its home—it is the Apple of Peru, with its blue-and-white flowers and its black seedcases—seeds that can lie dormant for decades, they do say. I am happy that these come back, and happy (although I do not bank on it) to see the tobacco plants return, especially #15, *Nicotiana sylvestris.*

I used to believe, in principle, that the only sunflower worth growing would be the traditional, and the tallest type. But I was converted—by Sarah Raven's catalogue, a short but growing and well-thought-out selection of seeds aimed for the flower arranger (see chapter 12 for the address)—to #16, *Helianthus annuus* "Valentine," with lemon-yellow petals and a dark center. What you lose in height (not much, admittedly) you gain in flower power. You must stake these things, or they fall over and uproot themselves.

#17, *Salvia sclarea*, Clary, is important for us in early summer, and seeds itself around, offering tall, pale bracts. You want hazy? It does hazy, sure. Hazy and tall is the Scotch Thistle, #18, *Onopordum acanthium*, brother to #19, the Milk Thistle, *Silybum marianum*. And may I mention another plant that "fires a gun": #20, *Lychnis chalcedonica*, Maltese Cross, for scarlet in the palette, which I failed to squeeze into the previous chapter?

THREE

FLOWERS
THAT HOP AROUND

ALL BUT THE TIDIEST, most obsessively controlling of gardeners look forward to those plants that hop around. At first they are placed near the front of the border. Next they find their way out onto the path, into the gravel or the cracks in the paving. And the first time this happens one thinks: Now my garden is beginning to show that extra panache—this is maturity in miniature, and these will be my signature plants.

They could be something special, they could be nothing out of the ordinary. At first I used to wonder what was the name of the tiny bronze clover-leaved oxalis, which you often see in front gardens. A "cosmopolitan weed," the dictionary calls it, *Oxalis corniculata*, the procumbent yellow sorrel. Soon I discovered I had acquired it anyway, along with another classic, the fern-leaved yellow fumitory, *Corydalis lutea*, which is so flattering to a new retaining wall. A third of these, the ivy-leaved toadflax, with its purple-and-yellow snapdragon flowers, soon followed unbidden.

Less commonly seen is #21, *Omphalodes linifolia* or Venus's Navelwort. Gray-leaved and with spikes of white flowers, this twelve-inch annual brings with it thoughts of *broderie anglaise*, white needlework on white, the underwear of the high-minded. The first sowing might be in spring, but at the end of its season the drying spikes are cut down and laid, in my garden, wherever we think we could do with some more of this charmer. The seeds ripen and fall out, and by autumn the new seedlings are showing. Gertrude Jekyll reckoned this for cutting.

Now, if this gray-and-white scheme were to need jazzing up with black, #22, *Viola tricolor* "Bowles' Black" is the unanswerable self-seeder. Irrefutably black when grown in isolation, it enjoys fooling around with other violas. Keen on bloodlines, are we? Then we should "rogue out" the less perfectly black seedlings. But to me the variations are all part of "the music of what happens." Another viola with the gift of profusely seeding itself is the purple-green-leaved *V. labradorica*, the Labrador violet.

True, serious blue: rightly is it said that a garden can't get enough of it. And it is a big mistake to suppose, in going for delphiniums, that the best must always be the tallest. Years ago, I bought at the supermarket a delphinium marked "Blue Pygmy." This must be #23, *Delphinium grandiflorum* "Blauer Zwerg." It seeded itself and has been coming back, in a raised bed, in gravel and between paving, ever since. A perennial that can behave like an annual, it survives winters in places like Siberia and Mongolia. There are other strains of *D. grandiflorum* should this one prove elusive. Another cutter for the small bouquet, this is a naturally short delphinium, not some perverse plant breeder's mean-minded fantasy.

For a very small California Poppy, #24, *Eschscholzia caespitosa* "Sundew": about the smallest poppy I have grown, and I have lost it through allowing it to be crowded out. But I shall try it again, sown in a raised bed in a warm spot, and next time without competition. The "Sundew" in its name denotes a particularly pale yellow strain, but I should be equally happy with the species.

For its foliage, and particularly for the way its variegated rosettes of thistle leaves keep growing through the winter months (the huge car-doon offers the same out-of-season interest), #25, *Galactites tomentosa* recommends itself. Don't think of moving a mature plant (should such be available). It doesn't like that. And don't, I beg you, be disappointed on viewing the plant in flower, because that (unusually enough) happens to be its worst time of the year. But you must let it flower, because you must let it seed itself around. The suggestion of milk in the name refers to the incomparable white veining of the leaves, which are tomentose (woolly) underneath.

Thrift next, that is #26, *Armeria maritima*, the Sea Pink, which, on cliff tops, is normally grazed or windswept to a close turf, but which in the garden grows into luxuriant hummocks. Ignore the opinion of the Reverend William Hanbury that the "withered heads and stalks will much injure the beauty of those in bloom, and have a dull, indolent and disagreeable look." You want those withered heads to seed themselves in the cracks, so that you can then chuck out the old cushions. "It is a foolish man dead-heads his thrift" (spurious old proverb).

Foolish, too, is the impulse to tidy up #27, *Pulsatilla vulgaris*, the Pasque Flower, for the seed heads are beautiful (like those of the clematis), and the ripe seed is best sown fresh, or allowed to spread itself around. Still, given a large enough supply, one would like to cut this rare (but not difficult) wildflower for the house.

#28, Chives, *Allium schoenoprasum*: obvious, yes, but it is better to be obvious (and have a supply of chives) than to be subtle (and purchase plastic packs at irritating prices). And, besides, it is traditional to have chives growing by the kitchen door.

A prolific corydalis, less frequently found than the yellow fumitory mentioned above is

#29, *C. cheilanthifolia.* The specific name means that it has leaves like the lip fern, *Cheilanthes.* Tinged bronze in spring, with yellow flowers, it participates in that clothing of the as-yet-unclad spaces, and is as welcome therefore as #30, *Erigeron mucronatus*, a Mexican Daisy, the quintessential plant for hopping around.

I admit that, with hummocks of thrift and clumps of chives and all the rest of these flowers growing among the paving around the back door, you need an almost Ethiopian agility when running in from the garden to answer the telephone. Cordless phones are the answer, not tidy paving.

FOUR

FLOWERS
FOR CUTTING

TASTE HAS CHANGED greatly over the last ten years, and the list of flowers we feel like growing reflects that change. Some of the change has been consciously campaigned for in the gardening press: there has been an entertaining running battle mounted by Christopher Lloyd against received wisdom and ghastly good taste, against the timid palette of so many gardens. At the same time, and perhaps less noticed, there is the effect of fashion in interior decorating.

If you look at what is proposed, in clever, design-conscious shops, as a flower vase today (indeed, if you look at the common colors of many modern household objects), it is not surprising that the flowers we would choose to fill these vases come from a different list from the ones we would have chosen for the home a few years ago. And it is inevitable that if a certain flower begins to look good in the house, it will in time begin to look good again in the garden.

The alternative hypothesis would be that we will have a range of city flowers, for deployment in interiors, and country flowers, for the great outdoors. This supposes that the modern designer's passion for brightly colored daisies such as gerberas will be confined to the city section of the brain, while old roses will continue to thrive in the country section. However, this is not happening. The same newspapers and magazines are read in city and country.

I well remember a gardening friend, ten years ago, saying gently and forgivingly, "Now, what's all *that* about?," gazing into a bed in which common marigolds had been allowed to get, perhaps, out of hand. But the common pot marigold can hold its own extremely well in a common modern vase. *Calendula officinalis* is the name, and I recommend as #31 the strain called "Indian Prince."

For a vivid illustration of this shift in floral taste, you can compare two books which would seem to be addressing the same subject.

The Flower Arranger's Garden by Rosemary Verey (Conran Octopus, 1989; paperback 2000) presents us with plans for borders and island beds which, without undue disturbance, can be plundered for the house. But you would have to be very clever to guess, just from looking at them, that these designs had been made with the flower arranger in mind. The emphasis is on shrubs and perennials, and only a handful of annuals makes its way into the list of essential flowers.

By comparison, *The Cutting Garden* by Sarah Raven (London: Frances Lincoln, 1996; New York: Reader's Digest, 1996) proposes a kind of design in which the function of the plot announces itself boldly. Flowers are planted in straight lines, as they might be in allotments, or in frank, comprehensible clumps. This is more than what the Americans sometimes call a posy patch: it could well constitute your whole garden. But if every flower is chosen with an eye to its usefulness for cutting, it follows—or it seems to follow—that the list of flowers will be different from those you would expect in a garden laid out without such a purpose in mind.

Many flowers mentioned earlier in this series come into such a scheme: basic, apparently simple-minded choices like cornflowers, nasturtiums, love-in-a-mist, forget-me-nots, sunflowers, and delphiniums. And perhaps, to some tastes, the list, when set out like that, might begin to look infantile. Who can imagine that it is sophisticated to grow snapdragons? Perhaps it is not. But when I first saw the buckets full of giant snapdragons for sale in New York, I wondered why I was not growing #32, *Antirrhinum majus,* in my garden. You need an F1 hybrid seed for the full three-foot scale.

Flowers that remind one of hot continental summers include the Mexican sunflower mentioned previously, *Tithonia rotundifolia,* which always brings back Giverny for me, and #33, *Cosmos bipinnatus* "Purity," the white version. We grow the crimson "Dazzler" as well. These we tend to dot around the borders, where they do especially happily in warm summers, as does the Spider Flower, #34, *Cleome spinosa*, available in purple, pink, and white. South America and the West Indies are where it is at home. It packs a mean thorn.

These plants earned their place in the garden long before the question of cutting them arose. And the same is true of that native of Texas and Louisiana #35, *Gaura lindheimeri*: you want to see it waving in the breeze, giving a pink shimmer to the border, long before you want—if indeed you do—to see it in a vase. But I would think twice before letting #36, the Zinnias, out of the posy patch. These are what you see grown in straight rows in France, and that is how they look good—or in a simple jug. Cactus-flowered are the ones we grow.

Always on the lookout for things to grow near roses, and hoping that they will be long-flowering, I was delighted last year with #37, *Salvia viridis* "Blue," from Sarah Raven's list.

The blue is in the bracts—brilliant Moroccan blue, the catalogue calls it, and puts it in the top ten for foliage. It will seed itself around, which is one reason I want it. Another reason is its flowering season—May to October. This used to be called *S. horminum*. That it lasts indefinitely in a vase is a prospect that gives me the horrors.

Sweet Scabious, #38, or *Scabiosa atropurpurea*, is by some called Egyptian rose, though, truth to tell, it is South African. One for the black garden, it grew generously for us. Among the numerous columbines, Chiltern Seeds is offering #39, *Aquilegia alpina* "Hensol Harebell," a particularly desirable blue. And if I were obliged to restrict myself to one Sweet Pea, #40 would be the one, listed by Sarah Raven as *Lathyrus matucana* (syn. "Cupani's original"), and "Cupani" in the addendum to the Chiltern catalogue. This pea was sent in 1699 from Sicily to the grammar school in Enfield, an auspicious start to a distinguished and influential career.

FIVE

THE
PERENNIAL PREJUDICE

IF YOU LOOK at the lists of gardening books in print, you will find that the volumes devoted to perennials notably outnumber those concerned with annuals and biennials. And if you look at the volumes devoted to annuals, you may well find that they are not really devoted to annuals at all but to bedding plants which may or may not be, strictly speaking, annuals.

And this fact has some significance. For part of the neglect of annuals in the gardening press may be put down to an ancient dislike of bedding plants, which were associated with badly run parks. According to this prejudice—that is what it has become—the foundation of good gardening is the abandoning of bedding plants in favor of perennials and shrubs. And according to a recent, more extreme version, the foundation of good gardening is the abandonment of everything (shrubs, annuals, bulbs, the lot) except perennials: the aim is to create vast perennial ecologies, prairies at the bottom of the garden.

Do you believe in prairies? They may prove an awesome undertaking, and perhaps in the end a somewhat boring prospect; a horror, potentially, if not done well. But then, the same applies to any gardening style.

My strong preference is for a garden, as it were, "open to all the talents"—and that is why

I always pay particular attention to the minority of garden writers who look seriously at annuals and biennials. This has nothing to do with bedding schemes (which I am very happy to see done well) but everything to do with getting to know and use the full range of possible plants available.

Some of these flowers are going to die on us after one (annuals) or two (biennials) years. If this fact is too dismaying to contemplate, you have an annuals problem. If the dismay derives simply from the thought that all your planting will have to be done over again, you are overlooking a range of obliging plants which will indeed come back, and in profusion. An obvious example is #41, the common Foxglove, *Digitalis purpurea*, which will seed itself and come back, being biennial, every other year, and will grow happily under trees and bushes. Excessive devotion to perennials would cut you off from this pleasure, as from the delights of #42, Honesty, *Lunaria annua.* Both the purple honesty and the pink foxglove have their white versions. Do you want to live without these? Do you want to live without honesty?

Another biennial which we allow to colonize a clump of blackthorns is the beautiful umbellifer #43, *Smyrnium perfoliatum,* Alexanders. When it is performing, the upper part of the plant turns a yellowy green, so that a drift of *Smyrnium* gives the illusion of a pool of sunlight in a wood.

A similar yellowy green is offered by another umbellifer, or annual herb for full sunlight, #44, Dill, or *Anethum graveolens.* It is a color found useful by hip florists, who also turn to a self-sowing perennial, #45, Lady's Mantle, or *Alchemilla mollis.* Chiltern Seeds offers a version of this called *A. mollis* "Robustica," which is the one for cut flowers.

And in the context of so much yellow, and such prolific self-sowing, I must mention a perennial member of the poppy family, *Chelidonium majus*, and its double version, #46, *C. majus* "Flore Pleno." *Chelidonium*, known as the Greater Celandine, is a flower of the hedgerow. My seed I collected outside Holy Trinity

Church, Brompton Road, London, beloved of evangelical city slickers (the church, that is). The flower may be too evangelical for some tastes: it certainly spreads the word.

If one was told of an annual which grew to around six feet, had flowers like pink coal scuttles, and smelt of 1950s hair oil, would the prospect be attractive? I like #47, *Impatiens glandulifera*, or, as Chiltern Seeds has it, *I. roylei*—Himalayan Balsam—well enough. It reminds me of the banks of the Wear in Durham, with its exploding seed capsules. But it is superprolific, and I should not mention it without saying that it is much best introduced into a wild part of the garden, if such is available.

Turn to that essential work of garden reference, *Annuals and Biennials* by Roger Phillips and Martyn Rix (London: Macmillan, 1999), and you will find eight pages with illustrations devoted to impatiens. And these are by no means all busy Lizzies (versions of *I. walleriana*) but include many yellow-flowered species from damp places in China, and some with no names yet.

Like the other volumes by Phillips and Rix, *Annuals and Biennials* shows photographs not only of the individual plants but also, in many cases, of the way these grow in their spectacular natural habitats, such as the Mojave Desert, Cape Province, or Himalayan foothills. One gets an idea—whether rightly or not—of the way these flowers might be persuaded to grow naturally in the garden.

Any flower can be made to look ridiculous, through ridiculous planting. One remembers the solemn way in which borders were edged with alternating plants of alyssum and lobelia. Yet #48, Sweet Alyssum, *Lobularia maritima*, grows happily enough when taken out of this context and allowed to seed itself quietly in some crack or other, at the foot of a wall, or in some paving. And I like finding #49, *Lobelia erinus*, growing where some pot or other once stood.

This is one way in which annuals make themselves a perennial feature of the garden. That is not to say that we should expect them all to oblige in the same way, to relieve us of the obligation to think things afresh. It is just that some flowers, such as the charming blue Oriental Woodruff, #50, *Asperula orientalis*, can be relied on to remember to renew themselves, even if we forget.

SIX

USEFUL AND
DECORATIVE HERBS

THIS BOOK BEGAN with the proposition that it might be a good idea to look at the kind of garden that could be made, on any site from a balcony upwards, using only a hundred packets of seed. I have so far avoided flowers which, although they could well in theory be raised from seed, are much better acquired as plants.

The point is not to make things harder. The

point, to recap, is to look at the flower garden at the beginning of the season as if it were a vegetable garden and ask simply: What do I want to grow this year? Forget design for a moment. Design has become a terrible, stupid, and expensive tyrant. The emphasis here is all on content. Such a flower garden should have the same beauty as an allotment. It says: This is what I felt like having this year.

If I feel like making myself an omelette *fines herbes*, I need equal quantities of finely chopped parsley, tarragon, chives, and chervil. But where do I get the chervil? It is the slenderest, most delicate and wilting of herbs, and I really must grow it if I am to have it. So, for this reason alone, Chervil takes its place as #51, *Anthriscus cerefolium*. Cow parsley's kid brother, it will make no great impact on the garden, but the garden is where you need to have it.

Chives have already appeared as #28 on this

list (as has Dill, #44). For tarragon I would purchase a plant. Parsley, #52, *Petroselinum crispum*, is of great interest in the flower garden, and by parsley I mean the curly-leaved traditional variety. On the allotment, when it runs to seed, it may seem a nuisance, but when it seeds itself near the kitchen door it is both handy and handsome. That green is beautiful. That leaf is beautiful in the border too.

Another herb which you have to grow from seed if you are to have it is #53, Summer Savory, *Satureja hortensis*. There is one thing to do with it (apart from various supposed medicinal uses with which I have no patience), but that one thing is excellent: it is served chopped with young fava beans, dressed with olive oil or butter. It is an annual, like chervil. Winter savory, *Satureja montana*, its perennial cousin, is a nice thing, but not really a substitute.

Sorrel, #54, *Rumex acetosa*, you will sometimes see in the shops, but packaged in such mean quantities one wonders what the vendors can possibly have in mind. This is a leaf that, on the slightest contact with heat, dissolves into a gunge. A handful, stewed in butter, reduces almost to nothing. This "nothing" fills an omelette, or gets added to a chicken stock for a sorrel soup. For those Jane Grigson–ish moments of summer, this is what you need. Again, the only practical way is from seed.

Lovage, *Levisticum officinale*, comes in as #55, although you may prefer to buy a small plant. It will stay with you, putting on a good six foot of growth in a year, before dying back. Like many of my favorite garden plants, it is an umbellifer, and it stands happily at the back of the flower border. The leaves are chopped into a salad when young—later in the season they will become too tough and strong-tasting. The flavor is like that of celery. The books say it goes in casseroles or stocks. Take my advice: it will easily overwhelm a stock. Used in a salad, it stands up very well to a strong dressing of anchovy, garlic, lemon, and olive oil. One is told to cut the stems back to provide a fresh supply of young leaves. But I like to have one or two salads in early summer, and then enjoy the plant for its gigantism.

What is Borage for? *Borago officinalis*, #56, is for distributing small flowers of pure sky blue around the garden. Admittedly, these blue flowers can look pretty in a salad, and there is the whole business of Pimm's. But does anybody really grow borage in order to add a cucumber taste to Pimm's, when a slice of cucumber would do the trick just as well? Borage is a really useful and friendly self-seeder, an incomparable addition to the garden's informal look. The white version may be thought to miss the point somewhat, but it, too, is welcome with us.

The various forms of culinary sage are normally grown from cuttings, as is rosemary, although the latter has seeded itself in my paving, and grown well there along with different thymes. And this reminds one that a plant such as the common Lavender, although easily bought, can be raised in quantity from seed, and that if you wanted a hedge of, for instance, #57, *Lavandula angustifolia* "Hidcote Blue," this would be one way of acquiring it.

In many respects the British climate is ideal for gardening, with its mild winters and not overhot summers. But for growing Basil you really need something fiercer than we can lay on. America is at an advantage here. When I bought a bunch of basil from a farmers' market in New York, I was stopped in the street, it was so spectacular: woody at the base, and pungent enough to leave its smell on your hands and clothes. *Ocimum basilicum*, #58, is the name; one can but try and try again. Chiltern Seeds lists almost twenty varieties.

Two final umbellifers for their garden beauty: Sweet Fennel, *Foeniculum vulgare*, in its bronze form, is #59, a plant to smell in the heat of a Mediterranean day; and #60, Sweet

Cicely, *Myrrhis odorata*, known once as cow chervil, sweet-humlock, sweets, or British myrrh—"very good for old people that are dull and without courage; it rejoiceth and comforteth the heart and increaseth their lust and strength" (dubious old herbal).

A likely story.

SEVEN

THE MICRO-MEADOW

 EVERYONE IS ATTRACTED by the idea of a meadow, or by the notion that meadow conditions can be imitated in the garden. A few discouraging but realistic remarks might be helpful. One thing I never see emphasized is that a meadow—a real meadow, that is—is a field with a product. If you have no use for the product, the hay, you are likely to have a problem with a meadow.

I recently read an admirable account of a garden grown largely for the benefit of insects. Every plant was rated according to the number and variety of insects it attracted. Towards the end, the author admitted that, finding it hard to compost the hay from her garden, she had the local council—that is, the local government authority—cart it away instead. But there must be something wrong with the ecology of this.

Another thing that sets my teeth on edge when meadow enthusiasts describe what they have done is the insistence that since meadow flowers grow best on poor soil, you should lower the fertility of your soil before you begin. So far, so justifiable. But they go on to say that, if necessary, you should remove the fertile topsoil before sowing your meadow-seed mixture.

I protest. Who are handing out this destructive advice, and who are listening to it? Who are carting away their fertile topsoil, and what are they finding underneath, when they have done so? What plants, what bulbs, what seeds are being carted away? And what have they done wrong?

It is only from the specialist point of view of the gardener that a meadow must have low fertility. An actual working meadow, which is supposed to grow a crop of grass for cattle, may have at least two obvious sources of fertility.

It may have clover. Does the meadow gardener propose to exclude clover from the mix, on the grounds that it introduces too much nitrogen into the soil?

The second source of fertility is, of course, animals. "Sheep eat the grass, then dung the ground for more," wrote that admirable poet George Herbert, describing a desirable aspect of providence. A meadow is grown for its hay. When that is cut, and the grasses have grown again, the field is grazed. Among the beneficial effects (from the point of view of the meadow gardener) of this grazing is the fact that the cattle tread the new seed into the ground. Indeed, one way in which you can turn a cultivated field into a meadow, and which we have practiced on my farm with some success, is to take the hay from another meadow and spread it over the target area, and then put cattle on it. The cattle both eat the hay (or not, if they don't feel like it) and tread it underfoot.

The easiest way to start a meadow is to take a field or patch of lawn and put it under a meadow regime: no fertilizers, pesticides, or herbicides, no animals to graze it, no mower to touch it before the first cut of the year—and this cut to come only after the seeds of the desirable wildflowers have been allowed to ripen. Meadows, like lawns, arise through management, and this is the basic management for a wildflower meadow. The results are to be appreciated over years, decades even.

In fields where fertilizers were once used, the effect will wear off reasonably quickly. Obviously, if the farmer was applying fertilizer annually, he was doing so because an annual application was necessary for the effects he wished to achieve (fertilizers are expensive). So the effect is reversible, to some extent at least. To make a wildflower meadow on such a site, it is better to try the new management system, and see where it leads.

An old, neglected field which I bought to add to the farm, and which I knew to contain many cowslips and perhaps some other interesting flowers, was (on professional advice) gone over once with a disc harrow, so that the surface of the soil was disturbed but the turf was not entirely destroyed. Then it was rolled assiduously, to produce a ground so firm that, we were instructed, a bicycle should not leave a track in it. Onto this firm surface we sowed our grass and wildflower mix. In the first year, the field was cut early, in order to stop unwanted annuals, such as thistles, from seeding. So it wasn't until the second year that we could really tell how successful our efforts had been.

It turned out that we were very successful indeed. The field retains its cowslips, which have spread fast, and some eccentricities from its former life—such as patches of daffodils. I should not be surprised one year to find orchids there, because they would certainly have been there in the past. And the way we are managing the field is designed to encourage them if they are there, as they are on other parts of the farm. Note that in all this we have made no attempt to eliminate the coarser grasses, either by plowing or by weed-killing or by (supposing this to have been feasible on a large scale) the removal of topsoil. The four meadows we have, each somewhat different in character and history, have been developed on the basis of what we found there in the first place.

This kind of perennial meadow is distinct from the vision you tend to see in blurry pastel photographs, in which poppies, cornflowers, and corn cockle give an "impressionist" effect. The annual flowers blooming in such fields are the weeds of wheat fields, and in order to bloom readily they need a wheat-field regime. But this implies annual plowing—and this is very far from the repertory of most gardeners.

However, what is possible—and much easier to achieve than a really satisfactory perennial wildflower meadow (which should be viewed as a long-term project)—is a micro-meadow of annual flowers, grown in a small patch. Two years ago, we did this, and the reaction of visitors was always at first to laugh at the small scale of our project: intended as a wheat field with traditional extras, it measured only six paces by two.

The wheat we took from a handful or two of mixed birdseed—a mistake, since such seed may often be heat-treated, which destroys its viability. The wildflowers came from a couple of packets of wildflower mix, available in any garden center, together with the things we particularly wanted: cornflowers (which have featured early in this list as #2); #61, *Agrostemma githago* or Corn Cockle; and #62, *Papaver rhoeas* or Field Poppy.

The ground was prepared in April and the seed mixture scattered over. In the early stages, some obvious weeds were removed, while others, like the purple-flowered wall fumitory, *Fumaria muralis*, were left. A dominant presence among the flowers, along with the cornflowers and poppies, was corn chamomile, *Anthemis arvensis*. In due course, we had a spectacular display, but little evidence of corn in our field.

Later, I was reading the introduction to *Annuals and Biennials*, the important book by Roger Phillips and Martyn Rix which I have already mentioned, when I came across this sentence: "Poppies, cornflowers, corn-cockle and *Nigella*, combined with some grasses, umbelliferae and white daisies, will make a fine scheme to recreate a neolithic Mediterranean cornfield." This was indeed what we had achieved, with just the sort of poor germination of grain that neolithic man might have expected in a bad year, but with compensating blooms of #63, *Leucanthemum vulgare*, or Ox-eye Daisy.

Chiltern Seeds offers #64, a Mixture of Annual Varieties, and #65, a Mixture of Perennial Varieties, which could serve as a basis for two such miniature schemes. Of interest as well is #66, its California Wildflower Mixture. Phillips and Rix go on to say: "Californian annuals include the wonderful blue and purple *Phacelia* and the pale blue *Nemophila*, as well as the different colours of Californian poppies. Lupins, clarkias and white *Oenothera* complete a grouping which could occur in California."

An article in the March 2001 issue of *The Garden*, the journal of the Royal Horticultural Society, reports on experiments with this kind of direct sowing. It recommends a thin layer of sand spread over the bed as a weed-suppressing mulch (the seeds being sown onto this sand), and it shows the difference between results with or without a modest use of slug pellets. The authors, Nigel Dunnett and James Hitchmough, calculate that to plant a square meter with herbacious perennial plants may cost one hundred times as much as using seed.

They tell us that topsoil in a typical garden will contain a "seed bank" of ten thousand seeds per square meter. These are waiting to germinate when the soil is disturbed. However, a layer of sand of between 5 and 10 millimeters—up to three-eighths of an inch—will reduce weed germination to manageable levels. A single application of slug pellets around the time of the germination of the seeds proved effective, and it was shown that these pellets did not have to be applied all over the sown plot, but only around the edges. Without slug pellets at all, the seedlings suffered 35 percent damage.

[EIGHT]

THE POPPY FESTIVAL

 WHAT REALLY GETS a regular garden going is not so much a plan as a craze, or a series of overlapping crazes. And when we are in the grips of the craze, we want to know everything there is to be known about a plant—how it appears in every variant, what can be done with it, what will make it happy. When the craze subsides, it may be that we can begin to think the unthinkable: to admit, for instance, that we are going to have to live without azaleas, or cut down on our hydrangea habit.

Something will normally survive these crazes, and whatever it is that survives them—whether it is a single species or a group of plants—should take its place among our permanent affections. Maybe a flower does not agitate us anymore in the way it used to, but that does not mean we have forgotten it, or become indifferent.

When I first began to put my garden together, it seemed to me that, within the garden, there should be a rose garden, and that somewhere around there should be as many types of iris as could be accommodated. Furthermore, so it seemed to me, there should be lilies in abundance. Obviously roses, irises, and lilies were the essential constituents of a flower garden.

So it seemed to me, and so it still seems! But it is years since I added a rose to the mixture, or even looked seriously at the rose catalogues. Irises and lilies are a different matter, for we keep adding to their number, and varying the approach to growing them: sometimes they have been scattered to all corners of the garden, sometimes grouped together, particularly if they are being grown to be cut.

Propagation by seed is not the first consideration in either case, although, given a little patience and space, and given the desire for a large number of lilies, some species are worth growing in this way. That great star of the genus, #67, *Lilium regale*, sows itself around in my garden to a modest degree, but in a manner that seems to suggest that one would be foolish to throw away the ripe seed heads. The Chiltern catalogue says it may flower in the second year from seed. But not nearly at full strength, in our experience. In three years, however, there it is.

A more prolific self-seeder, on the raised bed

where we grow it (for it is a small thing, best grown among small plants such as alpines), is *L. formosanum var. pricei.* This is a short-stemmed version of plain *L. formosanum*, which others recommend as a biennial, although we have yet to do well with it. Among several lily seeds, Chiltern offers #68, *L. formosanum* "Little Snow White," which must be the one we grow.

Still, in a garden envisaged as growing from a hundred packets of seed, neither lilies nor irises will be the star performing genus. The poppies have far more to offer—fragile though they may sometimes seem. That fragility is an illusion. The Spanish Poppy, #69, *Papaver rupifragum*, in what I call pale orange, may seem of feeble constitution, but it just hangs around the back door, returning year after year, looking after itself. We grow #70, *P. sendtneri*, in paving: it is pure white and miniature, and it does not insist on its native limestone (or that

altitude of nine thousand feet, which is sometimes inconvenient to arrange).

The field poppy (*P. rhoeas*) mentioned in the
previous chapter earns an honored place in the
garden in the strain called the "Shirley" poppy,
which, to be what the Reverend William Wilks
had in mind when he selected it, ought to be a
single flower in white, pink, or salmon. Modern
versions delight in their doubleness.

This kind of annual makes itself a perennial feature of the garden by reliably resowing its own patch, as does the tall, incomparable Opium Poppy, #71, *P. somniferum*, which comes in so many forms, single and double. "Black Peony" is one I would choose—almost at random. Nothing hangs on your decision in choosing between the opium poppies. The foliage will all be the same handsome glaucous blue-green. The range of colors—from white through red, pink, and purple—seems entirely appropriate to the plant. One is not more virtuous, or more likely to go to heaven, for preferring singles to doubles, or plain to cut-edged petals.

In all but the most specialized climates, there is no question of opium's being extracted from this poppy, nor is its cultivation illegal in the United States, where several seed companies offer it, and where it has been grown for over two centuries. (But check your state and local laws

before you plant.) In England it has been cultivated since the Bronze Age.

More and more often seen on sale is #72, the
Iceland Poppy, usually listed as *P. nudicaule*. Its
popularity represents a further triumph for the
color orange, for orange is what it does best—
a deeper, warmer orange than the California
poppy, which I listed as #4. The white version,
and the intermediate pastel shade, and the yellow are pleasant variants on the essential orange, the thing itself. This is a flower which
astonishes us by being good for cutting, when
you would think that it would wilt straight
away. (Dipping the cut ends in boiling water is
the trick.)

One associates poppies with full sunlight and
the heat of early summer, but their range in-
cludes the cool and shady. #73, *Meconopsis cambrica*, the yellow Welsh Poppy, and its orange
and scarlet variants are self-seeders for shade,

flowers that, like the chelidonium (which is also a kind of poppy), are expected to get on with it, furnishing shady walks and gravel paths. I would rave about the blue Himalayan meconopsis if I honestly—or plausibly—could claim to have grown it. Instead, on the blue theme, let me mention *Corydalis linstowiana*—for corydalis is often listed as a member of the Papaveraceae, an annual or biennial which has seeded itself under our roses, with pale-blue flowers. You would have to buy a plant to start it off.

Two prickly Mexican poppies, #74, *Argemone mexicana*, and #75, *A. pleiacantha*, the first with yellow, the second with white flowers (*A. grandiflora* "White Lustre" is its name in the Chiltern list), suggest themselves as candidates for a hot Mediterranean-style garden. Yet we grow the white one among our roses, which is where I first saw it at Mottisfont. No doubt in Mexican rose gardens they curse it as a weed.

NINE

CLIMBERS ON IMPULSE

AT THE START OF THIS BOOK,
I mentioned a garden I had
seen last summer in Manhattan,
which consisted of nothing more
than morning glories growing up a fire escape. I saw the remains of it again the other
day, high above Forty-third Street, the dead
vines washed gray against the dark metal-
work. If I had appreciated it and remembered
its location, no doubt I was one of many who

had enjoyed it and thought: That was a success.

Suppose it were a success not to be repeated. Suppose the instigator of this garden had simply thought, This year, I feel like seeing morning glories every morning, and for a summer had reveled in the triumph of the project—but the following year were to turn to something else. Would there be something wrong with that?

I imagine the flower forever having a particular association for the owner of this "garden"—this nondescript container dumped on a fire escape, which suddenly, and so satisfactorily, took off. Whatever the summer of 2000 meant would be summed up by the sight of #76, *Ipomoea tricolor* "Heavenly Blue."

To me it means sleeping under a trellis in Greece, but ipomoea is historically associated with Central America. A quick check in the Codex Badianus, an Aztec herbal now in the Vatican, gives us the fever flower, *Tontonquixo-*

chitl, and a recipe against hair loss: "Falling hair is checked by washing the head, and if the herb called *xiuhhamolli* is applied to it, ground and cooked in the urine of a dog or a stag, with tree frogs and the small animals *quatecolotl*" (apparently a kind of caterpillar).

What the codex fails to impart is the recipe for deriving LSD from *I. tricolor*, which was the standard Aztec hallucinogen. An illustration of the associative power of the flower is the fact that morning glory always lifts the heart, whereas the common white convolvulus (so very similar in form) always causes it to sink. I have not tried the white version of morning glory ("Pearly Gates") for that reason. There are reds on offer as well. *I. batatas*, as the name more than hints, is the sweet potato.

The smaller the garden, the greater the interest in extending it by means of climbers. Some small town houses have no garden at all, but the house itself has been interpreted as, first and foremost, a support for a rampant clematis or wisteria. I like these examples of horticultural excess very much, but where there is the opportunity to grow just a few more plants it is the smaller climbers that will attract the attention of the householder. They are less likely to crowd their neighbors out.

Early on, I mentioned the common nasturtium, *Tropaeolum majus*, grown in the courtyard of a Boston museum, massed in window boxes. The windows in question are extraordinary, having been transported from Venetian palazzi. The planting might have looked foolish had it been done with anything less than total conviction. As it was, with cascades of nasturtiums, one felt one was seeing the flower used properly for the first time.

An illusion, of course, that the self-confident can create. There are many other tropaeolums, including one that features in that useful book *Lost Crops of the Incas** T. tuberosum*, known to us in the form "Ken Aslet" (boil the tubers with meat), and to South Americans as *mashua*, a crop for high altitudes which (mark this, now) repels many insects and pathogens, and is handy for farmers who can't afford pesticides.

But the tropaeolum I am recommending from seed is #77, the delicate yellow-flowered *T. peregrinum*, Canary Creeper, which comes from Peru and Ecuador and is for us a half-hardy annual. Another with which we have had success in southern England is #78, *T. ciliatum*, a Chilean, which we have growing up a yew hedge, where in Scotland one would more likely see the wonderful flame nasturtium, *T. speciosum*.

*Board on Science and Technology for International Development, National Research Council (Washington, D.C.: National Academy Press, 1989).

Another Chilean/Peruvian, to pursue the theme, is #79, *Eccremocarpus scaber*, the Glory Flower, which is a perfect climber for the small garden since it can climb through a shrub without giving it too much hassle. Orange-and-red tubular flowers, bright and small, are its contribution. We also grow "Tresco Cream," which is presumably one of the constituents of Chiltern Seeds' offering, "Tresco" mixed. Listed as half-hardy, it is very likely to survive a town winter.

Returning to Mexico, we encounter #80, the astonishing *Rhodochiton atrosanguineum*, another tender vine, with blood-black flowers (as its specific name warns us to expect) and a surprisingly pronounced calyx. Its color is similar to that of the popular chocolate cosmos.

Here are two versions of flowers better known in nonclimbing forms: #81, *Dicentra scandens*, is a climbing version of Dutchman's Breeches, aka Bleeding Heart, but with yellow or white heart-shaped flowers. This is a Himalayan perennial. And #82, *Aconitum hemsleyanum*, is a Chinese climbing Monkshood, and

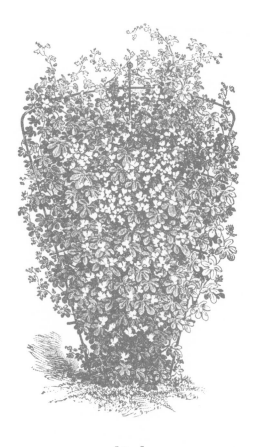

therefore presumably (I haven't tried it) poison-ous. The flowers are dark blue, as you'd expect.

Sweet peas I have mentioned earlier in the context of their great ancestor, *Lathyrus cupanii*. #83 is a blue-flowered pea, *L. sativus var. azureus*, known, the books tell me, as Riga or Dogtooth Pea. And since a mere two peas might sound stingy, I would add a packet of #84, Chiltern's Old-fashioned Sweet Peas, Mixed. The term "old-fashioned" in this context holds out an expectation of a better scent than that of more recent varieties, but scent is not my strong point.

Finally, #85, *Phaseolus coccineus*, is the Scarlet Runner Bean, a plant I am always happy to grow if not obliged to think about eating it. As a flower it is unanswerable, and that is all we need or wish to know about it.

TEN

FOR THE
TROPICAL LOOK

THE POPULAR and interesting tropical look that has returned to our gardens, giving a place for certain flamboyant plants which might previously have failed a taste test, is the result of an ingenious mix and match. It does not resemble a real tropical garden very closely. Rather, it gives an impression of lush colorfulness and rampant growth, using whatever plant material suits the fantasy of the designer.

When an actual habitation is established in your actual tropics, the first plants to surround the house will be economic staples such as coconut, banana, bamboo, and papaya. None of these will perform for us in their tropical varieties, although papaya grows so fast from seed it would be worth trying in the conservatory. Real bananas are always grown from offsets.

The first ornamental plants to grace an actual tropical garden are the same the whole world round (tropical gardens can pall after a while): bougainvillea, hibiscus, and some sort of impatiens will be sure evidence of human habitation. Orchids hanging under the eaves, or tied onto tree trunks, will show that the garden has passed stage one. But often this is as far as things will go. Barrio gardens are seldom very elaborate, just as cottage gardens, in the days of cottagers, were much less fancy than legend would suggest.

Two flowers of use in the temperate garden, both of which can be grown from seed, are widespread in the tropics.

The first is *Lantana camara*, a small shrub with bright flower heads in a mixture of red, orange, and yellow. A kind of verbena, it has become a roadside weed in the tropics. Thompson and Morgan offer #86, *Lantana camara* "Mixed Hybrids," whereas Chiltern Seeds has a dwarf version.

The second is #87, the familiar *Thunbergia alata*, Black-eyed Susan Vine, available from both catalogues, a small climber sold here in England for hanging baskets. The best easily available photo reference book for tropical flowers is the two-volume *Conservatory and Indoor Plants* by Roger Phillips and Martyn Rix (London: Pan, 1998; published in the United States as *The Random House Book of Indoor and Greenhouse Plants* [New York: Random House,

1997]), a work which is somewhat mislabeled, since it is full of photographs of plants in their natural habitats. Two pages of thunbergias here are enough to provoke the appetite for a flower, climbing or trailing, which turns out, surprisingly, to be an acanthus relative.

Fundamental to any genuine tropical look are the banana-like, large-leaved heliconias, cannas, and ginger lilies. The normal way would be to buy these as plants, but cannas in particular can be raised from seed. #88, *Canna indica*, Indian Shot, is offered by both catalogues. Cannas don't have to be grown in borders. In the tropics they grow in water very happily—for instance, at the edge of a pond—and this is where they can be placed during summers here. Cannas started from fresh seed collected in a garden last summer look fair to flower for us this year.

Last year a friend of mine planted a packet

of #89, *Melianthus major*, seed from Chiltern. Of the twelve seeds, ten germinated. She kept two plants, gave one to us, and sold the rest, thereby ending the year both popular and in profit. Melianthus is grown in these "tropical" schemes from its glaucous foliage. Left out of doors, it may well survive the winter but it will not flower: the English year does not offer enough heat for it.

But Phillips and Rix show us what it looks like flowering in California, with tall spikes of chocolate flowers in spring (August–September in its native South Africa). What gardeners in England have turned into a herbaceous perennial is by nature a tall, rangy shrub beloved of sunbirds. We are now experimenting with other members of the family, including *M. comosus* (Chiltern). They germinate easily.

Naranjilla, #90, another of the lost crops of the Incas I mentioned in the last chapter, will grow out of doors if given a good start in the greenhouse. *Solanum quitoense* (Chiltern) is its name, and you want it to grow six feet. But even if it doesn't get that far, it will interest you with its bright-purple-veined leaves. Supposing it to have ripened its golf-ball-sized fruit, you can spread the unstrained pulp on your Guatemalan-style cheesecake!

Another solanum, #91, goes under the name of Poroporo or Large Kangaroo Apple. This is *S. laciniatum*, a raffish, cut-leaved job with egg-shaped fruit, also edible. The whole solanum family seems to have this ambiguous, not entirely respectable, either edible or poisonous (or both, like the potato) character.

Distinctly poisonous is the Castor Oil Plant, #92, *Ricinus communis*, the source (if I am not mistaken) of the poison (ricin) in the famous umbrella murder by the KGB of a Bulgarian journalist in London not long ago. Mrs. M. Grieve, in *A Modern Herbal* (1931; Penguin reprint; Dover reprint, 1971; available in hypertext on the Web), gives a vivid Victorian account of a scientist inadvertently half killing himself with it. It is a Mediterranean plant which has been in English gardens for perhaps half a millennium, perhaps more, but that doesn't stop it from looking tropical. We have had best success with a variety called *gibsonii*.

Marvel of Peru, *Mirabilis jalapa*, #93, was deemed marvelous for producing different-colored flowers on the same plant. It gave its other name, Four O'Clock, to the family of Nyctaginaceae. Unless you can grow bougainvillea, which is improbable in England, you won't have many other Nyctaginaceae in your collection, so why not this easy subtropical weed?

A tropical-style border also featured in the March 2001 issue of *The Garden* features #94, *Rehmannia angulata*, the Chinese Foxglove. We grow this among the roses, where it does not look out of place. Along the same lines, and perhaps more exciting, #95 is *Isoplexis isabelliana* (Chiltern) or, from Thompson and Morgan, you could try *I. sceptrum*. These last three share a page in Phillips and Rix, *Conservatory and Indoor Plants*, vol. 2.

ELEVEN

AS AN
AFTERTHOUGHT

 LOOKING BACK on this list, which draws from flowers that have been grown from seed and enjoyed in my garden over the last ten years or so, I can see some surprising gaps. Wot, no dianthus? Neither the cottage pinks nor the lusher carnations? Well, we haven't got onto carnations, and our cottage pinks, of which we have many, have all been bought or given us as plants and propagated from cuttings. *Dianthus barbatus*, Sweet William, comes in at #96 as being, par excellence, the dianthus to grow from seed, as a biennial, among the roses.

I would have mentioned, had the seed been simpler to find, two small-flowered, long-stemmed Balkan types. *D. cruentus* and *D. giganteus*: the bloody and the gigantic, respectively. The Royal Horticultural Society encyclopedia is rude about the only yellow wild species, *D. knappii*, calling it "unattractive of habit," as if it picked its nose. But I like it, and I see the Chiltern catalogue has it and is enthusiastic. Then there are the ground-hugging alpine types, one of which, *D. deltoides*, the Maiden Pink, has spread happily by seed. Of this, a deep-scarlet variety called "Flashing Light" or "Leuchtfunk" surely earns its place, #97.

Of the many seeds spread by birds, not all are welcome, but some get left for amusement's sake. There are one or two bird-sown asparagus plants allowed to grow in the rose garden, on the grounds that, if asparagus fern looks right in a bridegroom's buttonhole, the thing itself can hardly look wrong among rosebushes. But I wouldn't defend this reasoning to the death.

When a truly distinguished plant adopts your garden, it is flattering. The wild spurge laurel, *Daphne laureola*, brought along by a friend who was digging a ditch nearby, has become a presence for us. One might think it wouldn't like our clay. One would be wrong. It turns up everywhere, a harmonious, low evergreen daphne. The handsome cousin of the cuckoo pint, #98, *Arum italicum var. pictum*, seems to find a place under every shrub, as a matter of course.

And then there was the question whether the Foxtail Lily, #99, the amazing, huge *Eremurus robustus*, would do for us what I had read it did in another rose garden (Hyde Hall, I think): seed itself and produce its eight-foot spikes of flowers among shrub roses. I wondered whether the leaves of the eremurus would get enough light in these conditions to thrive.

The answer is that the leaves, which have been heaving through the soil in enormous, almost worrying buds, all through March, get enough of a start in spring and early summer, before the competition shades them over. In nature, they die anyway before the plant flowers.

But one must have patience, or have other things to think about during the three or four years the seedlings take to grow to flowering size.

One should indeed have other things to think about—ninety-nine other things to think about once I have added #100, the Willow Gentian, *Gentiana asclepiadea*, to the list. I choose it as being not too choosy to be happy with me: a tallish thing, two feet or so, rather than the ground-hugging kind, happy in shade and almost any soil.

I think that this was the kind of gentian D. H. Lawrence had in mind when he wrote his poem "Bavarian Gentians," since he twice refers in the final version of the poem to the tallness of the stems (*G. bavarica*, the Bavarian gentian, is mat-forming and short). He speaks of "Bavarian gentians, tall and dark, but dark / darkening the daytime torch-like with the smoking blueness of Pluto's gloom . . ." And he cries, "Give me a flower on a tall stem, and three dark flames . . ." He was dying, and he considered it a privilege to have such flowers in the house.

Well, that's my list, and I have forgotten the euphorbias, but it is now too late to do anything about it. The closer you look, the worse the omissions will be, and this garden I have proposed—this reckless coming together of plants—will have faults enough for those who wish to find them. Where are the hellebores, the bulbs, the winter interest? Where are the shrubs? Where are the grasses? Where are the tree ferns?

Where are the tree ferns indeed? For the amount of the reader's money I have spent so far on this hypothetical garden—the packets of seed, some topsoil, the odd book—one could purchase perhaps one handsome tree fern and a pot to put it in. *And this might well be the best way forward.*

For about ten times the amount of money I have spent, one might install a small new off-the-peg "landscaped" garden in a new home. "Features" (paving, ponds, containers) cost money. Maturity (the grouping of plants for immediate impact and effect) costs money. And it is striking that some of the smallest gardens in Britain are the most expensive, per square meter, to achieve, and striking the amount of propaganda that comes at us, through television or through the gardening press, encouraging this level of expenditure.

I'm not in a position to lecture anyone about expenditure: my garden employs one gardener full-time and has benefited over the years from a great deal of part-time assistance. I regret none of the expenditure (even the heroic failures), as long as I think that the money was, in principle, well used. But even the most lavish gardener in Great Britain—as it were, the Duchess of Northumberland—would think twice about spending on the large scale at the same rate per square inch that the amateur urban gardener is encouraged to spend on a small back garden.

TWELVE

THE REST
OF THE KIT

 EVERY GARDEN can benefit from a reference library, but it does not have to be large. I have mentioned several times volumes in the Garden Plant Series, written by Roger Phillips and Martyn Rix, and published in Britain by Pan and in the United States by Random House. The single volume on *Annuals and Biennials*, the two on *Perennials*, and the one on *Bulbs*, taken together, offer a formidable photographic archive. The two volumes on *Indoor and Greenhouse Plants* are much more interesting than you might expect (if you don't have a conservatory). We grow many of the plants in these volumes out of doors. We await *Alpines*.

There is one general work, of great interest to anyone who has been intrigued at all by this book, called *Garden Flowers from Seed*, by Christopher Lloyd and Graham Rice, available from Timber Press. Mr. Rice has two other volumes on growing annuals, worth looking for.

I mentioned several times Sarah Raven's *Cutting Garden*, a catalogue available from Perch Hill Farm, Brightling, Robertsbridge, East Sussex TN32 5HP, England, or at *www.thecutting garden.com*. There is a book by Dr. Raven called *The Cutting Garden* (Reader's Digest, 1996), which I find has a good attitude. The two large seed catalogues I have referred to are the one I

have cited most often, Chiltern Seeds—not il-
lustrated, but extremely wide-ranging, and I
would say the seeds come cheap, from Bortree
Stile, Ulverston, Cumbria LA12 7PB, England,
or *www.chilternseeds.co.uk*; and Thompson and
Morgan Inc., whose U.S. address is P. O. Box
1308, Jackson, NJ 08527-0308; telephone
1-800-274-7333; fax 1-800-466-4769; or at
www.thompson-morgan.com. Also, in the United
States, Shepherd's Garden Seeds, 30 Irene
Street, Torrington, Connecticut 06790-6658;
telephone 1-800-444-6910; fax 1-860-626-0865;
or at *www.shepherdseeds.com*, offers many of the
varieties cited.

I restricted myself to such a small number of
sources in this book because I was interested to
keep my recommendations to a bare minimum,
but that does not mean that we do not use other
sources for seed, both large firms and small. Indeed, we are always on the lookout for rare and

unusual plants. One useful source is a botanical garden which runs a distribution scheme for seed. I am a member of the Friends of Oxford Botanic Garden (Rose Lane, Oxford OX1 4AZ).

As for equipment, there is a shed, and in this shed there is a bench on which most of the potting work is done. We have a small greenhouse, and some cold frames. The seeds are kept in an old fridge in the shed. We used to buy sacks of potting compost from the garden centers. But since we have space for a pile of what builders refer to as "sharp sand," we tend now to buy a sack of multipurpose compost, and mix it with sand and a little bonemeal, for our own potting mixture.

It is a long time since we bought plastic pots. When we have visitors and hold a plant sale, we ask if people have spares, and we find that our friends seem only too happy to get rid of old pots (just as we, in our turn, are only too happy

to get rid of wire coat hangers). So we have
sackfuls of old plastic pots. The seeds are started
off in these, rather than in seed trays, before being pricked out and potted on. The pricking out
is done with a sharpened length of bamboo.

Garden labels are an old problem. It is better to mark them in pencil rather than ink, which fades or gets washed off. Best for marking in pencil are the old-fashioned aluminum labels, but the magpies do find these attractive, and chuck them around. We use white plastic labels that will take pencil markings (not all of them do). A good watering can, with a fine rose or nozzle, makes an excellent Christmas gift, and one can always drop hints in that direction. And I hope that this book, too, will make a welcome gift.

WHEN RAISING
PLANTS FROM SEED

1. Do pay attention to the instructions on the packet, particularly the recommended months for sowing. Sowing seeds early or out of season is not always a good idea. Sometimes you get away with it, but not always.

2. Sow most seeds onto compost in four-inch pots, which give them a good depth for their roots. If the seeds are large, cover with compost roughly the same depth as the size of

the seed. Water with a fine, upturned rose.

3. Prick them out singly into individual pots when they are easy to handle. This varies with the type of seedling, but they should be showing their first set of true leaves.

4. Keep all pots and seedlings out of direct sunlight. If they dry out, you will lose them.

5. When removing seedlings from pots, if they are small, like lobelias, take a small chunk of compost with the dibble. If they are larger, remove the whole clump from the pot and it will fall apart.

6. When handling seedlings, always hold them by the leaves, not by the stem. Always treat them as gently as possible.

7. Water them with a solution of Cheshunt Compound (recommended) or other fungicide to stop them from damping off (being attacked by fungus). Use a fine, upturned rose.

8. Keep young plants in frost-free conditions— again, out of direct sunlight.

9. Gradually acclimatize them to cold weather: "harden them off" before planting them in the garden.

10. Potted-up seedlings and young plants should be given a weekly feed of Phostrogen (recommended) or other soluble fertilizer.

11. Always make sure a young plant is thoroughly watered before it is planted in the garden. A little bonemeal scattered in the hole will help, unless this encourages your dog to dig up the plant.

12. Forcefully remind your cat about the difference between seed trays and litter boxes.

THE SEED LIST

1. *Adonis aestivalis*, Pheasant's Eye (Ranunculaceae)
2. *Centaurea cyanus*, Cornflower (Asteraceae)
3. *Carthamus tinctorius*, Safflower (Asteraceae)
4. *Eschscholzia californica*, California Poppy (Papaveraceae)
5. *Tropaeolum majus*, Nasturtium (Tropaeolaceae)
6. *Tithonia rotundifolia* "The Torch," Mexican Sunflower (Asteraceae)

7. *Phacelia campanularia*, California Bluebell (Hydrophyllaceae)

8. *Oenothera biennis*, Evening Primrose (Onagraceae)

9. *Nigella damascena*, Love-in-a-Mist (Ranunculaceae)

10. *Myosotis sylvatica*, Forget-Me-Not (Boraginaceae)

11. *Angelica gigas* (Apiaceae)

12. *Ferula communis*, Giant Fennel (Apiaceae)

13. *Abutilon vitifolium* (Malvaceae)

14. *Nicandra physalodes*, Shoo-Fly Plant, Apple of Peru (Solanaceae)

15. *Nicotiana sylvestris* (Solanaceae)

16. *Helianthus annuus* "Valentine," Sunflower (Asteraceae)

17. *Salvia sclarea*, Clary (Lamiaceae)

18. *Onopordum acanthium*, Scotch Thistle (Asteraceae)

19. *Silybum marianum*, Milk Thistle (Asteraceae)

20. *Lychnis chalcedonica*, Maltese Cross (Caryophyllaceae)

21. *Omphalodes linifolia*, Venus's Navelwort (Boraginaceae)

22. *Viola tricolor* "Bowles' Black" (Violaceae)

23. *Delphinium grandiflorum* "Blauer Zwerg" (Ranunculaceae)

24. *Eschscholzia caespitosa* "Sundew" (Papaveraceae)

25. *Galactites tomentosa* (Asteraceae)

26. *Armeria maritima*, Thrift (Plumbaginaceae)

27. *Pulsatilla vulgaris*, Pasque Flower (Ranunculaceae)

28. *Allium schoenoprasum*, Chives (Alliaceae)

29. *Corydalis cheilanthifolia* (Fumariaceae)

30. *Erigeron mucronatus*, Mexican Daisy (Asteraceae)

31. *Calendula officinalis* "Indian Prince," Pot Marigold (Asteraceae)

32. *Antirrhinum majus*, Snapdragon (Scrophu-lariaceae)

33. *Cosmos bipinnatus* "Purity" (Asteraceae)

34. *Cleome spinosa*, Spider Flower (Cappari-daceae)

35. *Gaura lindheimeri* (Onagraceae)

36. *Zinnia* (Asteraceae)

37. *Salvia viridis* "Blue" (Lamiaceae)

38. *Scabiosa atropurpurea*, Sweet Scabious (Dipsacaceae)

39. *Aquilegia alpina* "Hensol Harebell" (Ra-nunculaceae)

40. *Lathyrus matucana* "Cupani," Sweet Pea (Papilionaceae)

41. *Digitalis purpurea*, Foxglove (Scrophulari-aceae)

42. *Lunaria annua*, Honesty (Brassicaceae)

43. *Smyrnium perfoliatum*, Alexanders (Api-aceae)

44. *Anethum graveolens*, Dill (Apiaceae)

45. *Alchemilla mollis* "Robustica," Lady's Mantle (Rosaceae)

46. *Chelidonium majus* "Flore Pleno," Greater Celandine (Papaveraceae)

47. *Impatiens glandulifera*, Himalayan Balsam (Balsaminaceae)

48. *Lobularia maritima*, Sweet Alyssum (Cruciferae)

49. *Lobelia erinus* (Campanulaceae)

50. *Asperula orientalis*, Oriental Woodruff (Rubiaceae)

51. *Anthriscus cerefolium*, Chervil (Apiaceae)

52. *Petroselinum crispum*, Parsley (Apiaceae)

53. *Satureja hortensis*, Summer Savory (Lamiaceae)

54. *Rumex acetosa*, Sorrel (Polygonaceae)

55. *Levisticum officinale*, Lovage (Apiaceae)

56. *Borago officinalis*, Borage (Boraginaceae)

57. *Lavandula angustifolia* "Hidcote Blue," Lavender (Lamiaceae)

58. *Ocimum basilicum*, Basil (Labiatae)

59. *Foeniculum vulgare* (bronze form), Sweet Fennel (Apiaceae)

60. *Myrrhis odorata*, Sweet Cicely (Apiaceae)

61. *Agrostemma githago*, Corn Cockle (Caryophyllaceae)

62. *Papaver rhoeas*, Field Poppy (Papaveraceae)

63. *Leucanthemum vulgare*, Ox-eye Daisy (Asteraceae)

64. Mixture of Annual Varieties

65. Mixture of Perennial Varieties

66. California Wildflower Mixture

67. *Lilium regale* (Liliaceae)

68. *Lilium formosanum var. pricei* (Liliaceae)

69. *Papaver rupifragum*, Spanish Poppy (Papaveraceae)

70. *Papaver sendtneri* (Papaveraceae)

71. *Papaver somniferum*, Opium Poppy (Papaveraceae)

72. *Papaver nudicaule*, Iceland Poppy (Papaveraceae)

73. *Meconopsis cambrica*, Welsh Poppy (Papaveraceae)

74. *Argemone mexicana* (Papaveraceae)

75. *Argemone pleiacantha* (Papaveraceae)

76. *Ipomoea tricolor* "Heavenly Blue" (Convolvulaceae)

77. *Tropaeolum peregrinum*, Canary Creeper (Tropaeolaceae)

78. *Tropaeolum ciliatum* (Tropaeolaceae)

79. *Eccremocarpus scaber*, Glory Flower (Bignoniaceae)

80. *Rhodochiton atrosanguineum* (Scrophulariaceae)

81. *Dicentra scandens* (Papaveraceae)

82. *Aconitum hemsleyanum*, Monkshood (Ranunculaceae)

83. *Lathyrus sativus var. azureus*, Riga or Dogtooth Pea (Papilionaceae)

84. Old-fashioned Sweet Peas, Mixed (Papilionaceae)

85. *Phaseolus coccineus*, Scarlet Runner Bean (Papilionaceae)

86. *Lantana camara* (Verbenaceae)

87. *Thunbergia alata*, Black-eyed Susan Vine (Acanthaceae)

88. *Canna indica*, Indian Shot (Cannaceae)

89. *Melianthus major* (Melianthaceae)

90. *Solanum quitoense*, Naranjilla (Solanaceae)

91. *Solanum laciniatum*, Poroporo or Large Kangaroo Apple (Solanaceae)

92. *Ricinus communis*, Castor Oil Plant (Euphorbiaceae)

93. *Mirabilis jalapa*, Marvel of Peru (Nyctaginaceae)

94. *Rehmannia angulata*, Chinese Foxglove (Scrophulariaceae)

95. *Isoplexis isabelliana* (Scrophulariaceae)

96. *Dianthus barbatus*, Sweet William (Caryophyllaceae)

97. *Dianthus deltoides* "Flashing Light" or "Leuchtfunk," Maiden Pink (Caryophyllaceae)

98. *Arum italicum var. pictum* (Araceae)

99. *Eremurus robustus*, Foxtail Lily (Liliaceae)

100. *Gentiana asclepiadea*, Willow Gentian (Gentianaceae)